Let's Wonder About Science
ACIDS AND BASES

J.M. Patten, Ed.D.

The Rourke Book Co., Inc.
Vero Beach, Florida 32964

PHOTO CREDITS
All photos © J.M. Patten

Library of Congress Cataloging-in-Publication Data

Patten, J.M., 1944-
    Acids and bases / J.M. Patten.
    p. cm. — (Let's wonder about science)
    Includes index.
    ISBN 1-55916-128-0
    1. Acids—Juvenile literature. 2. Bases (Chemistry)—Juvenile
literature. [1. Chemistry.] I. Title. II. Series: Patten, J.M., 1944-
Let's wonder about science.
QD477.P36 1995
546'.24—dc20   95-6213
                                     CIP
                                     AC

Printed in the USA

TABLE OF CONTENTS

WHAT IS SCIENCE?

Scientists usually talk about **acids** and **bases** together because they go together hand in hand. They are fascinating science and have amazing uses.

Weak acids are used in foods and helpful medicines. Strong acids burn skin and eat holes in metal. Bases are great for cleaning and even for brushing your teeth.

Do you wonder how all this works? Let's read all about it!

Children make good scientists because they wonder how things work.

HAND IN HAND—ACIDS AND BASES

Scientists put **compounds,** things made from two or more **elements,** into groups. This makes them easy to study and learn about. Let's look at two of these groups called acids and bases. They go together hand in hand.

Lemons taste sour because they contain citric acid.

Bases are foamy, soapy and slippery.

Everything in the acid group has some of the same **characteristics,** or things in common. Acids have a sour taste, and can sting and burn skin. Some acids can even eat through metal!

Bases have different characteristics from acids. They have a bitter taste and feel slippery or soapy.

Scientists warn us to be careful about things we study. Never touch or taste any substance to find out about it. That's very dangerous!

ACIDS HIDE IN LOTS OF PLACES

Have you ever had lemonade made with lemons just picked from the tree? Did you ever go strawberry picking? Do you grow tomatoes in a garden?

Let's wonder how tomatoes, strawberries and lemons are alike. It's not their shape, size or color. All three contain something scientists call acid.

You can find acids in lots of places. Some kinds of acids are in the foods we eat. Others are in plant foods called fertilizer. People use acids to make everything from car batteries to special lifesaving medicines.

Juice right from a grapefruit makes a great snack!

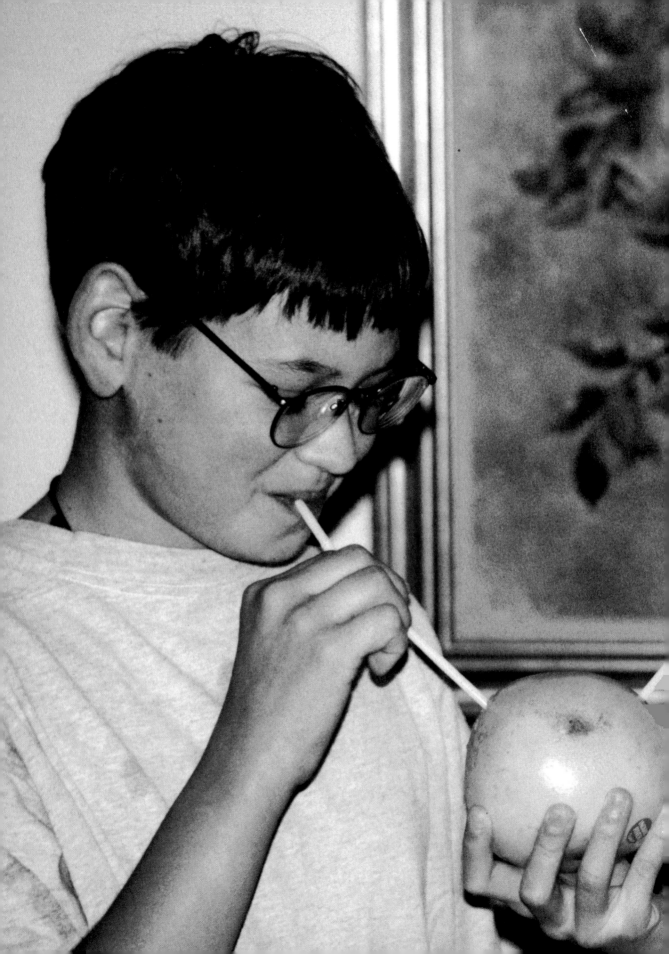

FOOD ACIDS HAVE PUCKER POWER

Lemons, limes, oranges, grapefruit and tangerines are called citrus fruit. They are citrus fruits because they all contain **citric acid.**

Citric acid has a pleasant, sour taste. It gives that special, fruity taste to some kinds of soda pop and foods. Lemonade tastes sour because of citric acid.

Citric acid has other jobs, too. It is used to make some kinds of inks, and to clean and shine steel. Many helpful medicines are made with citric acid.

Citric acid gives this Jell-O its lemony taste.

ASCORBIC ACID & ACETIC ACID

Ascorbic acid—in strawberries, tomatoes, citrus fruit and cabbage—is also called vitamin C. This vitamin is important for good health.

Vitamin C helps keep your bones and teeth strong, and it prevents gums from becoming sore and bleeding.

Ripe tomatoes are an excellent source of vitamin C.

There are many different types of vinegar, but they all contain acetic acid.

Early sailors who spent months and months on the ocean waters often developed bleeding gums and lost many teeth. After they learned to always eat foods containing ascorbic acid, this problem disappeared.

Vinegar is a sour liquid used in salad dressings, pickles and other foods. Vinegar contains **acetic acid.** That's what gives vinegar its special taste and makes it so good for preparing many foods.

DANGER! DANGER!

Acids found in foods are called *weak acids* because they will not harm us. The acid in a lemon may sting a small cut on your finger, but sucking a lemon or enjoying lemonade won't make you sick.

Other kinds of acids can be very strong and very dangerous. *Strong acids* will burn skin badly and even destroy metal. Strong acids are found in things like flashlight batteries. Never touch a battery that looks like it is leaking or crusty.

Batteries contain a strong and dangerous acid.

THE OPPOSITE OF AN ACID IS A BASE

Let's play opposites. Think of the word that means the opposite of each of the following:

Day

Long

Hot

Acid

Of course, your answers are night, short, cold, and, best of all, *base*.

The opposite of an acid is a substance called a base. Bases are found in lots of different things, too. They feel soapy and taste bitter.

Bases are found in many cleaning products, like car wash soap.

BASES ARE GREAT CLEANERS

Bases are used in many different kinds of cleaning products. Bases help to clean dirty clothes, dinner dishes—and even you.

Do you remember that bases feel slippery? That's why it's hard to pick up a wet bar of soap. Bath soap is a base.

It will take a lot of soap to clean this face!

Bases help us keep our clothes clean and fresh.

Some bases are very strong and very dangerous. They can eat through grease, hair and other gunk to unclog a stopped-up sink drain. They can also eat through you. Never smell, touch, taste or swallow a strange substance. It could be one of those strong bases.

BASES HELP BRUSH DECAY AWAY

Many bases help people instead of hurt them. Bases are used in medicines to settle upset stomachs.

Most toothpastes contain bases to help clean and protect your teeth. Bases are why toothpaste is bubbly or foamy in your mouth.

Shampoos for you and your dog are bases. Car wash soap, laundry and dish washing detergents, carpet cleaner and some spot removers are bases. Bases really clean up!

Strong acids and bases can be very dangerous. They can badly burn your eyes, your skin and the inside of your body. You're a good scientist who knows never to touch, smell, taste or swallow any unknown substance.

Soap suds are made from bases that really keep our friend smelling good.

GLOSSARY

acetic acid (ah SEET ik A sid) — the acid found in vinegar

acid (A sid) — a substance that tastes sour and burns skin

ascorbic acid (ah SKOR bik A sid) — also called vitamin C; found in strawberries, tomatoes and cabbage

base (BAYS) — the opposite of an acid; tastes bitter, and feels slippery and soapy

characteristic (kayr ak ter ISS tik) — a special quality or feature

citric acid (SIT rik A sid) — the acid found in citrus fruit

compound (KOM pownd) — a substance made up of two or more elements bonded together to make something new

element (EL uh ment) — atoms, or tiny parts, that make up all the different kinds of matter in the world

This citrus grove helps supply fruit rich in vitamin C.

INDEX